# The Path to Enlightenment: Discourses from Khuddaka Nikaya

*Bodhi Path Press*

GRAPEVINE INDIA

Published by

**GRAPEVINE INDIA PUBLISHERS PVT LTD**

www.grapevineindia.com

Delhi | Mumbai

email: grapevineindiapublishers@gmail.com

Ordering Information:

Quantity sales: Special discounts are available on quantity

purchases by corporations, associations, and others.

For details, reach out to the publisher.

First published by Grapevine India 2024

# CONTENTS

# FLOWERS

WHO SHALL overcome this earth, and the world of Yama, the lord of the departed, and the world of the gods? Who shall find out the plainly shown path of virtue, as a clever man finds the right flower?

The disciple will overcome the earth, and the world of Yama, and the world of the gods. The disciple will find out the plainly shown path of virtue, as a clever man finds the right flower.

He who knows that this body is like froth, and has learnt that it is as unsubstantial as a mirage, will break the flower-pointed arrow of Mara,3 and never see the king of death.

Death carries off a man who is gathering flowers, and whose mind is distracted, as a flood carries off a sleeping village.

Death subdues a man who is gathering flowers, and whose mind is distracted, before he is satiated in his pleasures.

As the bee collects nectar and departs without injuring the flower, or its color or scent, so let a sage dwell in his village.

Not the perversities of others, not their sins of commission or omission, but his own misdeeds and negligences should a sage take notice of.

Like a beautiful flower, full of color, but without scent, are the fine but fruitless words of him who does not act accordingly.

But, like a beautiful flower, full of color and full of scent, are the fine and fruitful words of him who acts accordingly.

As many kinds of wreaths can be made from a heap of flowers, so many good things may be achieved by a mortal when once he is born.

The scent of flowers does not travel against the wind, nor that of sandal-wood, or of Tagara and Mallika flowers,4 but the odor of good people travels even against the wind; a good man pervades every place.

Sandal-wood or Tagara, a lotus-flower, or a Vassikî, among these sorts of perfumes, the perfume of virtue is unsurpassed.

Mean is the scent that comes from Tagara and sandal-wood; the perfume of those who possess virtue rises up to the gods as the highest.

Of the people who possess these virtues, who live without thoughtlessness, and who are emancipated through true knowledge, Mara, the tempter, never finds the way.

As on a heap of rubbish cast upon the highway the lily will grow full of sweet perfume and delight, thus among those who are mere rubbish the disciple of the truly enlightened Buddha shines forth by his knowledge above the blinded worldling.

# DVAYATANUPASSANASUTTA:

## Contemplating Pairs

So I have heard. At one time the Buddha was staying near Savatthi in the Eastern Monastery, the stilt longhouse of Migara's mother. Now, at that time it was the sabbath—the full moon on the fifteenth day—and the Buddha was sitting in the open surrounded by the Sangha of monks. Then the Buddha looked around the Sangha of monks, who were so very silent. He addressed them:

"Suppose, mendicants, they questioned you thus: 'There are skillful teachings that are noble, emancipating, and lead to awakening. What is the real reason for listening to such teachings?' You should answer: 'Only so as to truly know the pairs of teachings.' And what pairs do they speak of?

'This is suffering; this is the origin of suffering': this is the first contemplation. 'This is the cessation of suffering; this is the practice that leads to the cessation of suffering': this is the second contemplation. When a mendicant meditates rightly contemplating a pair of teachings in this way—diligent, keen, and resolute—they can expect one of two results: enlightenment in the present life, or if there's something left over, non-return."

That is what the Buddha said. Then the Holy One, the Teacher, went on to say:

"There are those who don't understand suffering

and suffering's cause,

and where all suffering

ceases with nothing left over.

And they don't know the path

that leads to the stilling of suffering.

They lack the heart's release,

as well as the release by wisdom.

Unable to make an end,

they continue to be reborn and grow old.

But there are those who understand suffering

and suffering's cause,

and where all suffering

ceases with nothing left over.

And they understand the path

that leads to the stilling of suffering.

They're endowed with the heart's release,

as well as the release by wisdom.

Able to make an end,

they don't continue to be reborn and grow old."

"Suppose, mendicants, they questioned you thus: 'Could there be another way to contemplate the pairs?' You should say, 'There could.' And how could there be? 'All the suffering that originates is caused by attachment': this is one contemplation. 'With the utter cessation of attachment there is no origination of suffering': this is the second contemplation. When a mendicant meditates in this way they can expect enlightenment or non-return." Then the Teacher went on to say:

"Attachment is the source of suffering

in all its countless forms in the world.

When an ignorant person builds up attachments,

that idiot returns to suffering again and again.

So let one who understands not build up attachments,

contemplating the birth and origin of suffering."

"Suppose, mendicants, they questioned you thus: 'Could there be another way to contemplate the pairs?' You should say, 'There could.' And how could there be? 'All the suffering that originates is caused by ignorance': this is one contemplation. 'With the utter cessation of ignorance there is no origination of suffering': this is the second contemplation. When a mendicant meditates in this way they can expect enlightenment or non-return." Then the Teacher went on to say:

"Those who journey again and again,

transmigrating through birth and death;

they go from this state to another,

destined only for ignorance.

For ignorance is the great delusion

because of which we have long transmigrated.

Those beings who have arrived at knowledge

do not proceed to a future life."

"'Could there be another way?' ... And how could there be? 'All the suffering that originates is caused by choices': this is one contemplation. 'With the utter cessation of choices there is no origination of suffering': this is the second contemplation. When a mendicant meditates in this way they can expect enlightenment or non-return." Then the Teacher went on to say:

"All the suffering that originates

is caused by ignorance.

With the cessation of choices,

there is no origination of suffering.

Knowing this danger,

that suffering is caused by choices;

through the stilling of all choices,

and the stopping of perceptions,

this is the way suffering ends.

For those who truly know this,

rightly seeing, knowledge masters,

the astute, understanding rightly,

having overcome Mara's bonds,

do not proceed to a future life."

"'Could there be another way?' ... And how could there be? 'All the suffering that originates is caused by consciousness': this is one contemplation. 'With the utter cessation of consciousness there is no origination of suffering': this is the second contemplation. When a mendicant meditates in this way they can expect enlightenment or non-return." Then the Teacher went on to say:

"All the suffering that originates

is caused by consciousness.

With the cessation of consciousness,

there is no origination of suffering.

Knowing this danger,

that suffering is caused by consciousness,

with the stilling of consciousness a mendicant

is hungerless, extinguished."

"'Could there be another way?' … And how could there be? 'All the suffering that originates is caused by contact': this is one contemplation. 'With the utter cessation of contact there is no origination of suffering': this is the second contemplation. When a mendicant meditates in this way they can expect enlightenment or non-return." Then the Teacher went on to say:

"Those mired in contact,

swept down the stream of rebirths,

practicing the wrong way,

are far from the ending of fetters.

But those who completely understand contact,

who, understanding, delight in peace;

by comprehending contact

they are hungerless, extinguished."

"'Could there be another way?' … And how could there be? 'All the suffering that originates is caused by feeling': this is one contemplation. 'With the utter cessation of feeling there is no origination of suffering': this is the second contemplation. When a mendicant meditates in this way they can expect enlightenment or non-return." Then the Teacher went on to say:

"Whatever is felt

internally and externally—

whether pleasure or pain

as well as what's neutral—

having known this as suffering,

deceptive, falling apart,

one sees them vanish as they're experienced again and again:

that's how to understand them.

With the ending of feelings, a mendicant

is hungerless, extinguished."

"'Could there be another way?' … And how could there be? 'All the suffering that originates is caused by craving': this is one contemplation. 'With the utter cessation of craving there is no origination of suffering': this is the second contemplation. When a mendicant meditates in this way they can expect enlightenment or non-return." Then the Teacher went on to say:

"Craving is a person's partner

as they transmigrate on this long journey.

They go from this state to another,

but don't escape transmigration.

Knowing this danger,

that craving is the cause of suffering—

rid of craving, free of grasping,

a mendicant would wander mindful."

"'Could there be another way?' … And how could there be? 'All the suffering that originates is caused by grasping': this is one contemplation. 'With the utter cessation of grasping there is no origination of suffering': this is the second contemplation. When a mendicant meditates in this way they can expect enlightenment or non-return." Then the Teacher went on to say:

"Grasping is the cause of continued existence;

one who exists falls into suffering.

Death comes to those who are born—

this is the origination of suffering.

That's why with the end of grasping,

the astute, understanding rightly,

having directly known the end of rebirth,

do not proceed to a future life."

"'Could there be another way?' … And how could there be? 'All the suffering that originates is caused by instigating karma': this is one contemplation. 'With the utter cessation of instigation there is no origination of suffering': this is the second contemplation. When a mendicant meditates in this way they can expect enlightenment or non-return." Then the Teacher went on to say:

"All the suffering that originates

is caused by instigating karma.

With the cessation of instigation,

there is no origination of suffering.

Knowing this danger,

that suffering is caused by instigating karma,

having given up all instigation,

one is freed with respects to instigation.

For the mendicant with peaceful mind,

who has cut off craving for continued existence,

transmigration through births is finished;

there are no future lives for them."

"'Could there be another way?' ... And how could there be? 'All the suffering that originates is caused by sustenance': this is one contemplation. 'With the utter cessation of sustenance there is no origination of suffering': this is the second contemplation. When a mendicant meditates in this way they can expect enlightenment or non-return." Then the Teacher went on to say:

"All the suffering that originates

is caused by sustenance.

With the cessation of sustenance,

there is no origination of suffering.

Knowing this danger,

that suffering is caused by sustenance,

completely understanding all sustenance,

one is independent of all sustenance.

Having rightly understood the state of health,

through the ending of defilements,

using after reflection, firm in principle,

a knowledge master cannot be reckoned."

"'Could there be another way?' ... And how could there be? 'All the suffering that originates is caused by perturbation': this is one contemplation. 'With the utter cessation of perturbation there is no origination of suffering': this is the second contemplation. When a mendicant meditates in this way they can expect enlightenment or non-return." Then the Teacher went on to say:

"All the suffering that originates

is caused by perturbation.

With the cessation of perturbation,

there is no origination of suffering.

Knowing this danger,

that suffering is caused by perturbation,

that's why, having relinquished perturbation,

and stopped making karmic choices,

imperturbable, free of grasping,

a mendicant would wander mindful."

"'Could there be another way?' ... And how could there be? 'For the dependent there is agitation': this is the first contemplation. 'For the independent there's no agitation': this is the second contemplation. When a mendicant meditates in this way they can expect enlightenment or non-return." Then the Teacher went on to say:

"For the independent there's no agitation.

The dependent, grasping,

goes from this state to another,

without escaping transmigration.

Knowing this danger,

the great fear in dependencies,

independent, free of grasping,

a mendicant would wander mindful."

"'Could there be another way?' ... And how could there be? 'Formless states are more peaceful than states of form': this is the first contemplation. 'Cessation is more peaceful than formless states': this is the second contemplation. When a mendicant meditates in this way they can expect enlightenment or non-return."

Then the Holy One, the Teacher, went on to say:

"There are beings in the realm of luminous form,

and others stuck in the formless.

Not understanding cessation,

they return in future lives.

But the people who completely understand form,

not stuck in the formless,

released in cessation—

they are destroyers of death."

"'Could there be another way?' … And how could there be? 'What this world—with its gods, Maras, and Brahmas, this population with its ascetics and brahmins, its gods and humans—focuses on as true, the noble ones have clearly seen with right wisdom to be actually false': this is the first contemplation. 'What this world focuses on as false, the noble ones have clearly seen with right wisdom to be actually true': this is the second contemplation. When a mendicant meditates in this way they can expect enlightenment or non-return." Then the Teacher went on to say:

"See how the world with its gods

imagines not-self to be self;

habituated to name and form,

imagining this is truth.

For whatever you imagine it is,

it turns out to be something else.

And that is what is false in it,

for the ephemeral is deceptive by nature.

Extinguishment has an undeceptive nature,

the noble ones know it as truth.

Having comprehended the truth,

they are hungerless, extinguished."

"Suppose, mendicants, they questioned you thus: 'Could there be another way to contemplate the pairs?' You should say, 'There could.' And how could there be? 'What this world—with its gods, Maras, and Brahmas, this population with its ascetics and brahmins, its gods and humans—focuses on as happiness, the noble ones have clearly seen with right wisdom to be actually suffering': this is the first contemplation. 'What this world focuses on as suffering, the noble ones have clearly seen with right wisdom to be actually happiness': this is the second contemplation. When a mendicant meditates rightly contemplating a pair of teachings in this way—diligent, keen, and resolute—they can expect one of two results: enlightenment in the present life, or if there's something left over, non-return. That is what the Buddha said. Then the Holy One, the Teacher, went on to say:

"Sights, sounds, tastes, smells,

touches, and thoughts, the lot of them—

they're likable, desirable, and pleasurable

as long as you can say that they exist.

For all the world with its gods,

this is what they agree is happiness.

And where they cease

is agreed on as suffering for them.

The noble ones have seen as happiness

the ceasing of identity.

This insight by those who see

contradicts the whole world.

What others say is happiness

the noble ones say is suffering.

What others say is suffering

the noble ones know as happiness.

See, this teaching is hard to understand,

it confuses the ignorant.

There is darkness for the shrouded;

blackness for those who don't see.

But the good are open;

like light for those who see.

Though close, they do not understand,

those fools inexpert in the teaching.

They're mired in desire to be reborn,

flowing along the stream of lives,

mired in Mara's sway:

this teaching isn't easy for them to understand.

Who, apart from the noble ones,

is qualified to understand this state?

When they've rightly understood it,

they become extinguished without defilements."

That is what the Buddha said. Satisfied, the mendicants were happy with what the Buddha said. And while this discourse was being spoken, the minds of sixty mendicants were freed from defilements by not grasping.

# KASIBHARADVAJASUTTA:

## With Bharadvaja the Farmer

So I have heard.  At one time the Buddha was staying in the land of the Magadhans in the Southern Hills near the brahmin village of Ekanaḷa.  Now at that time the brahmin Bharadvaja the Farmer had harnessed around five hundred plows, it being the season for sowing.  Then the Buddha robed up in the morning and, taking his bowl and robe, went to where Bharadvaja the Farmer was working.  Now at that time Bharadvaja the Farmer was distributing food.  Then the Buddha went to where the distribution was taking place and stood to one side.

Bharadvaja the Farmer saw him standing for alms  and said to him,  "I plough and sow, ascetic, and then I eat.  You too should plough and sow, then you may eat."

"I too plough and sow, brahmin, and then I eat."  "I don't see Master Gotama with a yoke or plow or plowshare or goad or oxen, yet he says:  "I too plough and sow, brahmin, and then I eat."

Then Bharadvaja the Farmer addressed the Buddha in verse:

"You claim to be a farmer,

but I don't see your plough.

If you're a farmer, declare to me:

so that we can recognize a brahmin."

"Faith is my seed, austerity my rain,

and wisdom is my yoke and plough.

Conscience is my pole, mind my strap,

mindfulness my plowshare and goad.

Guarded in body and speech,

I restrict my intake of food.

I use truth as my scythe,

and gentleness is my release.

Energy is my beast of burden,

transporting me to a place of sanctuary.

It goes without turning back

where there is no sorrow.

That's how to do the farming

that has the Deathless as its fruit.

When you finish this farming

you're released from all suffering."

Then Bharadvaja the Farmer filled a large bronze dish with milk-rice and presented it to the Buddha: "Eat the milk-rice, Master Gotama, you are truly a farmer. For Master Gotama does the farming that has the Deathless as its fruit."

"Food enchanted by a spell isn't fit for me to eat.

That's not the principle of those who see, brahmin.

The Buddhas reject things enchanted with spells.

Since there is such a principle, brahmin, that's how they live.

Serve with other food and drink

the consummate one, the great hermit,

with defilements ended and remorse stilled.

For he is the field for the seeker of merit."

"Then, Master Gotama, to whom should I give the milk-rice?" "Brahmin, I don't see anyone in this world—with its gods, Maras, and Brahmas, this population with its ascetics and brahmins, its gods and humans—who can properly digest this milk-rice, except for the Realized One or one of his disciples. Well then, brahmin, throw out the milk-rice where there is little that grows, or drop it into water that has no living creatures."

So Bharadvaja the Farmer dropped the milk-rice in water that had no living creatures. And when the milk-rice was placed in the water, it sizzled and hissed, steaming and fuming. Suppose there was an iron cauldron that had been heated all day. If you placed it in the water, it would sizzle and hiss, steaming and fuming. In the same way, when the milk-rice was placed in the water, it sizzled and hissed, steaming and fuming.

Then Bharadvaja the Farmer, shocked and awestruck, went up to the Buddha, bowed down with his head at the Buddha's feet, and said, "Excellent, Master Gotama! Excellent! As if he were righting the overturned, or revealing the hidden, or pointing out the path to the lost, or lighting a lamp in the dark so people with good eyes can see what's there, Master Gotama has made the teaching clear in many ways. I go for refuge to Master Gotama, to the teaching, and to the mendicant Sangha. Sir, may I receive the going forth, the ordination in the

Buddha's presence?"

And Bharadvaja the Farmer received the going forth, the ordination in the Buddha's presence. Not long after his ordination, Venerable Bharadvaja, living alone, withdrawn, diligent, keen, and resolute, soon realized the supreme end of the spiritual path in this very life. He lived having achieved with his own insight the goal for which gentlemen rightly go forth from the lay life to homelessness. He understood: "Rebirth is ended; the spiritual journey has been completed; what had to be done has been done; there is no return to any state of existence." And Venerable Bharadvaja became one of the perfected.

# PURALASA (SUNDARIKABHARADVAJA) SUTTA:

## With Bharadvaja of Sundarika on the Sacrificial Cake

So I have heard. At one time the Buddha was staying in the Kosalan lands on the bank of the Sundarika river. Now at that time the brahmin Bharadvaja of Sundarika was serving the sacred flame and performing the fire sacrifice on the bank of the river Sundarika. Then he looked all around the four directions, wondering, "Now who might eat the leftovers of this offering?" He saw the Buddha meditating at the root of a certain tree with his robe pulled over his head. Taking the leftovers of the offering in his left hand and a pitcher in the right he approached the Buddha.

When he heard Sundarika's footsteps the Buddha uncovered his head. Sundarika thought, "This man is shaven, he is shaven!" And he wanted to turn back. But he thought, "Even some brahmins are shaven. Why don't I go to him and ask about his birth?" Then Sundarika the brahmin went up to the Buddha and said to him, "Sir, in what caste were you born?"

Then the Buddha addressed Sundarika in verse:

"I am no brahmin, nor am I a prince,

nor merchant nor anything else.

Fully understanding the clan of ordinary people,

I wander in the world owning nothing, reflective.

Clad in my cloak, I wander without home,

my hair shorn, quenched.

Since I'm unburdened by youngsters,

it's inappropriate to ask me about clan."

"Actually sir, when brahmins meet they politely

ask each other whether they are brahmins."

"Well, if you say that you're a brahmin,

and that I am not,

I shall question you on the Gayatri Mantra,

with its three lines and twenty-four syllables."

"On what grounds have hermits and men,

aristocrats and brahmins here in the world

performed so many different sacrifices to the gods?"

"During a sacrifice, should a past master, a knowledge master,

receive an oblation, it profits the donor, I say."

"Then clearly my oblation will be profitable,"

said the brahmin,

"since I have met such a knowledge master.

It's because I'd never met anyone like you

that others ate the sacrificial cake."

"So then, brahmin, since you have approached me

as a seeker of the good, ask.

Perhaps you may find here someone intelligent,

peaceful, unclouded, untroubled, with no need for hope."

"Master Gotama, I like to sacrifice

and wish to perform a sacrifice. Please advise me,

for I do not understand

where an oblation is profitable; tell me this."

"Well then, brahmin, lend an ear, I will teach you the Dhamma.

Don't ask about birth, ask about conduct;

for any wood can surely generate fire.

A steadfast sage, even though from a low class family,

is a thoroughbred checked by conscience.

Tamed by truth, fulfilled by taming,

a complete knowledge master who has completed the spiritual journey—

that is where a brahmin seeking merit

should bestow a timely offering as sacrifice.

Those who have left sensuality behind, wandering homeless,

self-controlled, straight as a shuttle—

that is where a brahmin seeking merit

should bestow a timely offering as sacrifice.

Those freed of greed, with senses stilled,

like the moon released from the eclipse—

that is where a brahmin seeking merit

should bestow a timely offering as sacrifice.

They wander the world unimpeded,

always mindful, calling nothing their own—

that is where a brahmin seeking merit

should bestow a timely offering as sacrifice.

Having left sensuality behind, wandering triumphant,

knowing the end of rebirth and death,

extinguished and cool as a lake:

the Realized One is worthy of the sacrificial cake.

Good among the good, far from the bad,

the Realized One has infinite wisdom.

Unsullied in this world and the next:

the Realized One is worthy of the sacrificial cake.

In whom dwells no deceit or conceit,

rid of greed, unselfish, with no need for hope,

with anger eliminated, quenched,

a brahmin rid of sorrow's stain:

the Realized One is worthy of the sacrificial cake.

He has given up the mind's home,

and has no possessions at all.

Not grasping to this world or the next:

the Realized One is worthy of the sacrificial cake.

Serene, he has crossed the flood,

and has understood the teaching with ultimate view.

With defilements ended, bearing his final body:

the Realized One is worthy of the sacrificial cake.

In whom desire to be reborn, and caustic speech

are cleared and ended, they are no more;

that knowledge master, everywhere free:

the Realized One is worthy of the sacrificial cake.

They've escaped their chains, they're chained no more,

among those caught in conceit he is free of conceit;

he has fully understood suffering with its field and ground:

the Realized One is worthy of the sacrificial cake.

Not relying on hope, seeing seclusion,

well past the views proclaimed by others.

In him there are no supporting conditions at all:

the Realized One is worthy of the sacrificial cake.

He has comprehended all things, high and low,

cleared them and ended them, so they are no more.

Peaceful, freed in the ending of grasping:

the Realized One is worthy of the sacrificial cake.

He sees the utter ending of rebirth's fetter,

and has swept away all manner of desire.

Pure, stainless, immaculate, flawless:

the Realized One is worthy of the sacrificial cake.

Not seeing himself in terms of a self,

he is stilled, upright, and steadfast.

Imperturbable, kind, wishless:

the Realized One is worthy of the sacrificial cake.

He harbors no delusions within at all,

he has insight into all things.

He bears his final body,

attained to the state of grace, the supreme awakening.

That's how the purity of a spirit is defined:

the Realized One is worthy of the sacrificial cake."

"Let my oblation be a true offering,

since I have found such a knowledge master!

I see Brahma in person! Accept my offering, Blessed One:

please eat my sacrificial cake."

"Food enchanted by a spell isn't fit for me to eat.

That's not the principle of those who see, brahmin.

The Buddhas reject things enchanted with spells.

Since there is such a principle, brahmin, that's how they live.

Serve with other food and drink

the consummate one, the great hermit,

with defilements ended and remorse stilled.

For he is the field for the seeker of merit."

"Please, Blessed One, help me understand:

now that I have encountered your teaching,

when I look for someone during a sacrifice,

who should eat the religious donation of one like me?"

"One who is rid of aggression,

whose mind is unclouded,

who is liberated from sensual pleasures,

and who has dispelled dullness.

One who has erased boundaries and limits,

expert in birth and death,

a sage, blessed with sagacity.

When such a person comes to the sacrifice,

get rid of your scowl!

Honor them with joined palms,

and venerate them with food and drink,

and in this way your religious donation will succeed."

"The Buddha is worthy of the sacrificial cake,

he is the supreme field of merit,

Recipient of gifts from the whole world,

what's given to the worthy one is very fruitful."

Then Sundarika the brahmin said to the Buddha, "Excellent, Master Gotama! Excellent! As if he were righting the overturned, or revealing the hidden, or pointing out the path to the lost, or lighting a lamp in the dark so people with good eyes can see what's there, Master Gotama has made the teaching clear in many ways. I go for refuge to Master Gotama, to the teaching, and to the mendicant Sangha. Sir, may I receive the going forth, the ordination in the Buddha's presence?" And the brahmin Sundarika Bharadvaja received the going forth, the ordination in the Buddha's presence. And soon after, he became one of the perfected.

# MAGHASUTTA:

## With Magha

So I have heard.  At one time the Buddha was staying near Rajagaha, on the Vulture's Peak Mountain.  Then the brahmin student Magha approached the Buddha and exchanged greetings with him.  When the greetings and polite conversation were over, he sat down to one side,  and said to the Buddha:

"I'm a giver, Master Gotama, a donor; I am bountiful and committed to charity. I seek wealth in a principled manner,  and with that legitimate wealth I give to one person, to two, three, four, five, six, seven, eight, nine, ten, twenty, thirty, forty, fifty, a hundred people or even more. Giving and sacrificing like this, Master Gotama, do I accrue much merit?"

"Indeed you do, student. A giver or donor who is bountiful and committed to charity, who seeks wealth in a principled manner,  and with that legitimate wealth gives to one person, or up to a hundred people or even more, accrues much merit." Then Magha addressed the Buddha in verse:

"I ask the bountiful Gotama,"

said Magha,

"wearing an ochre robe, wandering homeless.

Suppose a lay donor who is committed to charity

makes a sacrifice seeking merit, looking for merit.

Giving food and drink to others here,

how is their offering purifed?"

"Suppose a lay donor who is committed to charity,"

replied the Buddha,

"makes a sacrifice seeking merit, looking for merit,

giving food and drink to others here:

such a one would succeed due to those who are worthy of donations."

"Suppose a lay donor who is committed to charity,"

said Magha,

"makes a sacrifice seeking merit, looking for merit,

giving food and drink to others here:

explain to me who is worthy of donations."

"Those who wander the world unattached,

consummate, restrained, owning nothing:

that is where a brahmin seeking merit

should bestow a timely offering as sacrifice.

Those who have cut off all fetters and bonds,

tamed, liberated, untroubled, with no need for hope:

that is where a brahmin seeking merit

should bestow a timely offering as sacrifice.

Those who are released from all fetters,

tamed, liberated, untroubled, with no need for hope:

that is where a brahmin seeking merit

should bestow a timely offering as sacrifice.

Having given up greed, hate, and delusion,

with defilements ended, the spiritual journey completed:

that is where a brahmin seeking merit

should bestow a timely offering as sacrifice.

Those in whom dwells no deceit or conceit,

with defilements ended, the spiritual journey completed:

that is where a brahmin seeking merit

should bestow a timely offering as sacrifice.

Those rid of greed, unselfish, with no need for hope,

with defilements ended, the spiritual journey completed:

that is where a brahmin seeking merit

should bestow a timely offering as sacrifice.

Those not fallen prey to cravings,

who, having crossed the flood, live unselfishly:

that is where a brahmin seeking merit

should bestow a timely offering as sacrifice.

Those with no craving at all in the world

to any form of existence in this life or the next:

that is where a brahmin seeking merit

should bestow a timely offering as sacrifice.

Those who have left sensuality behind, wandering homeless,

self-controlled, straight as a shuttle:

that is where a brahmin seeking merit

should bestow a timely offering as sacrifice.

Those freed of greed, with senses stilled,

like the moon released from the eclipse:

that is where a brahmin seeking merit

should bestow a timely offering as sacrifice.

Those peaceful ones free of greed and anger,

for whom there are no destinies, being rid of them in this life:

that is where a brahmin seeking merit

should bestow a timely offering as sacrifice.

They've given up rebirth and death completely,

and have gone beyond all doubt:

that is where a brahmin seeking merit

should bestow a timely offering as sacrifice.

Those who live as their own island,

everywhere free, owning nothing:

that is where a brahmin seeking merit

should bestow a timely offering as sacrifice.

Those here who know this to be true:

'This is my last life, there are no future lives':

that is where a brahmin seeking merit

should bestow a timely offering as sacrifice.

A knowledge master, loving absorption, mindful,

who has reached awakening and is a refuge for many:

that is where a brahmin seeking merit

should bestow a timely offering as sacrifice."

"Clearly my questions were not in vain!"

said Magha,

"The Buddha has explained to me who is worthy of donations.

You are the one here who knows this to be true,

for truly you understand this matter.

Suppose a lay donor who is committed to charity

makes a sacrifice seeking merit, looking for merit,

giving food and drink to others here:

explain to me how to accomplish the sacrifice."

"Sacrifice, and while doing so,"

replied the Buddha,

"be clear and confident in every way.

Sacrifice is the ground standing upon which

the sacrificer sheds their flaws.

One free of greed, rid of anger,

developing a heart of limitless love,

spreads that limitlessness in every direction,

ever diligent day and night."

"Who is purified, freed, awake?

How can one go to the Brahma realm oneself?

I do not know, so please tell me when asked,

for the Buddha is the Brahma I see in person today!

To us you are truly the equal of Brahma.

Splendid One, how is one reborn in the Brahma realm?"

"One who accomplishes the sacrifice with three modes,"

replied the Buddha,

"such a one would succeed due to those who are worthy of donations.

Sacrificing like this, one rightly committed to charity

is reborn in the Brahma realm, I say."

When he had spoken, the student Magha said to the Buddha, "Excellent, Master Gotama! Excellent! … From this day forth, may Master Gotama remember me as a lay follower who has gone for refuge for life."

# UDAYAMANAVAPUCCHA:

## The Questions of Udaya

"To the meditator, rid of hopes,"

said Venerable Udaya,

"who has completed the task, is free of defilements,

and has gone beyond all things,

I have come in need with a question.

Tell me the liberation by enlightenment,

the smashing of ignorance."

"The giving up of both ,"

replied the Buddha,

sensual desires and aversion;

the dispelling of dullness,

and the cessation of remorse.

Pure equanimity and mindfulness,

preceded by investigation of principles—

this, I declare, is liberation by enlightenment,

the smashing of ignorance."

"What fetters the world?

What explores it?

With the giving up of what

is extinguishment spoken of?"

"Delight fetters the world.

Thought explores it.

With the giving up of craving

extinguishment is spoken of."

"For one living mindfully,

how does consciousness cease?

We've come to ask the Buddha;

let us hear what you say."

"Not taking pleasure in feeling

internally and externally—

for one living mindfully,

that's how consciousness ceases."

# UPOSATHASUTTA

## Sabbath

So I have heard. At one time the Buddha was staying near Savatthi in the Eastern Monastery, the stilt longhouse of Migara's mother. Now, at that time it was the sabbath, and the Buddha was sitting surrounded by the Saṅgha of monks.

And then, as the night was getting late, in the first watch of the night, Venerable Ananda got up from his seat, arranged his robe over one shoulder, raised his joined palms toward the Buddha and said, "Sir, the night is getting late. It is the first watch of the night, and the Saṅgha has been sitting long. Please, sir, may the Buddha recite the monastic code to the mendicants." But when he said this, the Buddha kept silent.

For a second time, as the night was getting late, in the middle watch of the night, Ananda got up from his seat, arranged his robe over one shoulder, raised his joined palms toward the Buddha and said, "Sir, the night is getting late. It is the first watch of the night, and the Saṅgha has been sitting long. Please, sir, may the Buddha recite the monastic code to the mendicants." But for a second time the Buddha kept silent.

For a third time, as the night was getting late, in the last watch of the night, as dawn stirred, bringing joy to the night, Ananda got up from his seat, arranged his robe over one shoulder, raised his joined palms toward the Buddha and said, "Sir, the night is getting late. It is the last watch of the night and dawn stirs, bringing joy to the night. Please, sir, may the Buddha recite the monastic code to the mendicants." "Ananda, the assembly is not pure."

Then Venerable Mahamoggallana thought, "Who is the Buddha talking about?" Then he focused on comprehending the minds of everyone in the Saṅgha. He saw that unethical person, of bad qualities, filthy, with suspicious behavior, underhand, no true ascetic or spiritual practitioner—though claiming to be one—rotten inside, corrupt, and depraved, sitting in the middle of the Saṅgha. When he saw him he got up from his seat, went up to him and said, "Get up, reverend. The Buddha has seen you. You can't live in communion with the mendicants." But when he said this, that person kept silent.

For a second time and a third time, he asked that monk to leave. But for a third time that person kept silent.

Then Venerable Mahamoggallana took that person by the arm, ejected him out the gate, and bolted the door. Then he went up to the Buddha, and said to him, "I have ejected that person. The assembly is pure. Please, sir, may the Buddha recite the monastic code to the mendicants." "It's incredible, Moggallana, it's amazing, how that silly man waited to be taken by the arm!"

Then the Buddha said to the mendicants, "From this day forth, mendicants, I will not perform the sabbath or recite the monastic code. Now you should perform the sabbath and recite the monastic code. It's impossible, mendicants, it can't happen that a Realized One could recite the monastic code in an impure assembly.

Seeing these eight incredible and amazing things the demons love the ocean. What eight?

The ocean gradually slants, slopes, and inclines, with no abrupt precipice. This is the first thing the demons love about the ocean.

Furthermore, the ocean is consistent and doesn't overflow its boundaries. This is the second thing the demons love about the ocean.

Furthermore, the ocean doesn't accommodate a corpse, but quickly carries it to the shore and strands it on the beach. This is the third thing the demons love about the ocean.

Furthermore, when they reach the ocean, all the great rivers—that is, the Ganges, Yamuna, Aciravati, Sarabhu, and Mahi—lose their names and clans and are simply considered 'the ocean'. This is the fourth thing the demons love about the ocean.

Furthermore, for all the world's streams that reach it, and the rain that falls from the sky, the ocean never empties or fills up. This is the fifth thing the demons love about the ocean.

Furthermore, the ocean has just one taste, the taste of salt. This is the sixth thing the demons love about the ocean.

Furthermore, the ocean is full of many kinds of treasures, such as pearls, gems, beryl, conch, quartz, coral, silver, gold, rubies, and emeralds. This is the seventh thing the demons love about the ocean.

Furthermore, many great beings live in the ocean, such as leviathans, leviathan-gulpers, leviathan-gulper-gulpers, demons, dragons, and fairies. In the ocean there are life-forms a hundred leagues long, or even two hundred, three hundred, four hundred, or five hundred leagues long. This is the eighth thing the demons love about the ocean. Seeing these eight incredible and amazing things the demons love the ocean.

In the same way, seeing eight incredible and amazing things, mendicants, the mendicants love this teaching and training. What eight?

The ocean gradually slants, slopes, and inclines, with no abrupt precipice. In the same way in this teaching and training the penetration to enlightenment comes from gradual training, progress, and practice, not abruptly. This is the first thing the mendicants love about this teaching and training.

The ocean is consistent and doesn't overflow its boundaries. In the same way, when a training rule is laid down for my disciples they wouldn't break it even for the sake of their own life. This is the second thing the mendicants love about this teaching and training.

The ocean doesn't accommodate a corpse, but quickly carries it to the shore and strands it on the beach. In the same way, the Saṅgha doesn't accommodate a person who is unethical, of bad qualities, filthy, with suspicious behavior, underhand, no true ascetic or spiritual practitioner—though claiming to be one—rotten inside, corrupt, and depraved. But they quickly gather and expel them. Even if such a person is sitting in the middle of the Saṅgha, they're far from the Saṅgha, and the Saṅgha is far from them. This is the third thing the mendicants love about this teaching and training.

Furthermore, when they reach the ocean, all the great rivers—that is, the Ganges, Yamuna, Aciravati, Sarabhu, and Mahi—lose their names and clans and are simply considered 'the ocean'. In the same way, when they go forth from the lay life to homelessness, all four castes—aristocrats, brahmins, merchants, and workers— lose their former names and clans and are simply considered 'Sakyan ascetics'. This is the fourth thing the mendicants love about this teaching and training.

For all the world's streams that reach it, and the rain that falls from the sky, the ocean never empties or fills up. In the same way, though several mendicants become fully extinguished through the natural principle of extinguishment, without anything left over, the natural principle of extinguishment never empties or fills up. This is the fifth thing the mendicants love about this teaching and training.

The ocean has just one taste, the taste of salt. In the same way, this teaching and training has one taste, the taste of freedom. This is the sixth thing the mendicants love about this teaching and training.

The ocean is full of many kinds of treasures, such as pearls, gems, beryl, conch, quartz, coral, silver, gold, rubies, and emeralds. In the same way, this teaching and training is full of many kinds of treasures, such as the four kinds of mindfulness meditation, the four right efforts, the four bases of psychic power, the five faculties, the five powers, the seven awakening factors, and the noble eightfold path. This is the seventh thing the mendicants love about this teaching and training.

Many great beings live in the ocean, such as leviathans, leviathan-gulpers, leviathan-gulper-gulpers, demons, dragons, and fairies. In the ocean there are life-forms a hundred leagues long, or even two hundred, three hundred, four hundred, or five hundred leagues long. In the same way, great beings live in this teaching and training, and these are those beings. The stream-enterer and the one practicing to realize the fruit of stream-entry. The once-returner and the one practicing to realize the fruit of once-return. The non-returner and the one practicing to realize the fruit of non-return. The perfected one, and the one practicing for perfection. This is the eighth thing the mendicants love about this teaching and training. Seeing these eight incredible and amazing things, the mendicants love this teaching and training."

Then, understanding this matter, on that occasion the Buddha expressed this heartfelt sentiment:

"The rain saturates things that are covered up; it doesn't saturate things that are open. Therefore you should open up a covered thing, so the rain will not saturate it."

# ARDOUR

This was said by the Lord, said by the Arahant, so I heard:

"Bhikkhus, a bhikkhu who is without ardour and without fear of wrongdoing is incapable of attaining enlightenment, incapable of attaining Nibbana, incapable of attaining the supreme security from bondage. But a bhikkhu who has ardour and fear of wrongdoing is capable of doing so."

This is the meaning of what the Lord said. So in regard to this it was said:

One who is not ardent, reckless,

Lazy, and of little vigour,

Full of lethargy and torpor,

Shameless and without respect—

Such a bhikkhu cannot attain

Enlightenment which is supreme.

But a mindful and discerning meditator,

Ardent, scrupulous, and diligent,

Having severed the fetters of birth and decay,

Can attain for himself right here and now

Enlightenment which is supreme.

This too is the meaning of what was said by the Lord, so I heard.

# NOT DECEIVING (1)

This was said by the Lord, said by the Arahant, so I heard:

"Bhikkhus, this holy life is not lived for the sake of deceiving people, for the sake of cajoling people, for the sake of profiting in gain, honour, and fame, nor with the idea, 'Let people know me thus.' This holy life, bhikkhus, is lived for the sake of restraint and abandoning."

This is the meaning of what the Lord said. So in regard to this it was said:

The Lord taught a holy life

Not based on tradition,

For restraint and abandoning,

Leading to and merging in Nibbana.

This is the path followed by the great,

Pursued by the lofty sages.

Those who enter that course

As taught by the Enlightened One,

Heeding the Teacher's instruction,

Will make an end of suffering.

This too is the meaning of what was said by the Lord, so I heard.

# NOT DECEIVING (2)

This was said by the Lord, said by the Arahant, so I heard:

"Bhikkhus, this holy life is not lived for the sake of deceiving people, for the sake of cajoling people, for the sake of profiting in gain, honour, and fame, nor with the idea, 'Let people know me thus.' This holy life, bhikkhus, is lived for the sake of direct knowledge and full understanding."

This is the meaning of what the Lord said. So in regard to this it was said:

The Lord taught a holy life

Not based on tradition,

For knowledge and understanding,

Leading to and merging in Nibbana.

This is the path followed by the great,

Pursued by the lofty sages.

Those who enter that course

As taught by the Enlightened One,

Heeding the Teacher's instruction,

Will make an end of suffering.

This too is the meaning of what was said by the Lord, so I heard.

# HAPPINESS

This was said by the Lord, said by the Arahant, so I heard:

"Bhikkhus, possessing two things a bhikkhu lives here and now with much pleasure and happiness and is properly motivated for the destruction of the taints. What are the two things? Being moved by a sense of urgency on occasions for urgency, and, being moved, making a proper endeavour. These, bhikkhus, are the two things, possessing which, a bhikkhu lives here and now with much pleasure and happiness and is properly motivated for the destruction of the taints."

This is the meaning of what the Lord said. So in regard to this it was said:

A wise person should be urgently moved

On occasions that make for urgency;

As an ardent discerning bhikkhu

He should investigate with wisdom.

One living ardent thus,

Of peaceful conduct, not proud,

Practising tranquillity of mind,

May attain the destruction of suffering.

This too is the meaning of what was said by the Lord, so I heard.

# OFTEN OCCURRING THOUGHTS

This was said by the Lord, said by the Arahant, so I heard:

"Bhikkhus, two thoughts often occur to the Tathagata, the Arahant, the Fully Enlightened One: the thought of security (for beings) and the thought of solitude.

"The Tathagata, bhikkhus, is one who delights in and enjoys non-ill will. As the Tathagata delights in and enjoys non-ill will, this thought often occurs to him: 'By this behaviour I do not oppress anyone either frail or firm.' The Tathagata, bhikkhus, is one who delights in and enjoys solitude. As the Tathagata delights in and enjoys solitude, this thought often occurs to him: 'What is unwholesome has been abandoned.'

"Therefore, bhikkhus, I say, you too must live delighting in and enjoying non-ill will. As you so live this thought will often occur to you: 'By this behaviour we do not oppress anyone either frail or firm.'

"Bhikkhus, you too must live delighting in and enjoying solitude. As you so live this thought will often occur to you: 'What is unwholesome? What has not been abandoned? What have we abandoned?'"

This is the meaning of what the Lord said. So in regard to this it was said:

Two thoughts occur to him,

The Tathagata, the Awakened One

Who endured what is beyond endurance:

Security (for beings) was the first thought spoken of,

Solitude was the second announced.

The dispeller of darkness, gone beyond,

The great sage who has reached attainment,

Become a master, freed from taints,

Who has crossed over entirely,

Released by the destruction of craving—

That sage bears his final body,

And having left behind Mara, I say,

He has gone beyond decay.

As one standing on a mountain peak

Might see all round the people down below,

So having ascended the Dhamma-palace,

The vastly wise one, all-seeing,

Views the people of the world.

The sorrowless one views below

Those still immersed in sorrow,

Overwhelmed by birth and decay.

This too is the meaning of what was said by the Lord, so I heard.

# DHAMMA-TEACHINGS

This was said by the Lord, said by the Arahant, so I heard:

"There are, bhikkhus, two successive Dhamma-teachings of the Tathagata, the Arahant, the Fully Enlightened One. What are the two? 'See evil as evil'— this is the first Dhamma-teaching. 'Having seen evil as evil, be rid of it, be detached from it, be freed from it'—this is the second Dhamma-teaching. These, bhikkhus, are the two successive Dhamma-teachings of the Tathagata, the Arahant, the Fully Enlightened One."

This is the meaning of what the Lord said. So in regard to this it was said:

Regard the ordered words he spoke,

The Tathagata, the Awakened One,

Compassionate for all beings,

And the two things he proclaimed:

"See what is evil" is one,

The other "Be detached from it."

With a mind become detached from evil

You will make an end of suffering.

This too is the meaning of what was said by the Lord, so I heard.

# VIGILANCE

This was said by the Lord, said by the Arahant, so I heard:

"Bhikkhus, a bhikkhu should be vigilant; he should live mindful, clearly comprehending, concentrated, happy and calm, and should know when it is suitable to cultivate those things that are wholesome. Bhikkhus, for a bhikkhu who is vigilant and living thus, one of two fruits is to be expected: final knowledge here and now or, there being some residual defilement, the state of non-returning."

This is the meaning of what the Lord said. So in regard to this it was said:

You vigilant ones hear this:

Wake up, you who are asleep!

Vigilance is better than sleep:

There is no fear for the vigilant.

One who is vigilant and mindful,

Comprehending and concentrated,

Joyful and calm in his thoughts,

By rightly investigating the Dhamma

With unified mind, will in time

Destroy the darkness of ignorance.

Therefore be devoted to vigilance,

An ardent, discerning, meditative bhikkhu.

Having severed the fetter of birth and decay,

One may here and now attain

Enlightenment which is supreme.

This too is the meaning of what was said by the Lord, so I heard.

# ELEMENTS

This was said by the Lord, said by the Arahant, so I heard:

"Bhikkhus, there are these three elements. What three? The form element, the formless element, and the element of cessation. These are the three."

This is the meaning of what the Lord said. So in regard to this it was said:

By fully understanding the form element

Without getting stuck in the formless,

They are released into cessation

And leave Death far behind them.

Having touched with his own person

The deathless element free from clinging,

Having realized the relinquishment of clinging

His taints all gone,

The Fully Enlightened One proclaims

The sorrowless state that is void of stain.

This too is the meaning of what was said by the Lord, so I heard.

# MORE PEACEFUL

This was said by the Lord, said by the Arahant, so I heard:

"Bhikkhus, the formless is more peaceful than the form realm, and cessation is more peaceful than the formless."

This is the meaning of what the Lord said. So in regard to this it was said:

Those beings who reach the form realm

And those established in the formless,

If they do not know cessation

Come back to renewal of being.

Those who fully understand forms

Without getting stuck in the formless,

Are released into cessation

And leave Death far behind them.

Having touched with his own person

The deathless element free from clinging,

Having realized the relinquishment of clinging,

His taints all gone,

The Fully Enlightened One proclaims

The sorrowless state that is void of stain.

This too is the meaning of what was said by the Lord, so I heard.

# FALLING AWAY

This was said by the Lord, said by the Arahant, so I heard:

"Three things, bhikkhus, lead to the falling away of a learner bhikkhu. What are the three? Here, a learner bhikkhu enjoys activity, is fond of activity, enjoys indulging in activity. He enjoys gossip, is fond of gossip, enjoys indulging in gossip. He enjoys sleep, is fond of sleep, enjoys indulging in sleep. These are the three things that lead to the falling away of a learner bhikkhu.

"Three things, bhikkhus, protect a learner bhikkhu from falling away. What are the three? Here, a learner bhikkhu does not enjoy activity, is not fond of activity, does not enjoy indulging in activity. He does not enjoy gossip, is not fond of gossip, does not enjoy indulging in gossip. He does not enjoy sleep, is not fond of sleep, does not enjoy indulging in sleep. These are the three things that protect a learner bhikkhu from falling away."

This is the meaning of what the Lord said. So in regard to this it was said:

A bhikkhu who enjoys activity,

Restless, fond of gossip and sleep,

Will never be able to attain

Enlightenment which is supreme.

Thus let him restrict his duties,

Give up sloth and restlessness;

Such a bhikkhu can attain

Enlightenment which is supreme.

This too is the meaning of what was said by the Lord, so I heard.

Unwholesome Thoughts

This was said by the Lord, said by the Arahant, so I heard:

"Bhikkhus, there are these three kinds of unwholesome thoughts. What three? A thought concerned with not being despised; a thought concerned with gain, honour, and fame; a thought concerned with involvement in the affairs of others. These, bhikkhus, are the three kinds of unwholesome thoughts."

This is the meaning of what the Lord said. So in regard to this it was said:

One concerned with not being despised,

With gain, honour, and esteem,

And who delights in companionship

Is far from the destruction of fetters.

But having abandoned sons and herds

Family life and possessions,

Such a bhikkhu can attain

Enlightenment which is supreme.

This too is the meaning of what was said by the Lord, so I heard.

# JOYOUS UTTERANCES

This was said by the Lord, said by the Arahant, so I heard:

"Bhikkhus, among the devas these three joyous utterances are proclaimed from time to time upon certain occasions. What three?

"At the time when a noble disciple, having had his hair and beard shaved off and having clothed himself in the yellow robe, intends going forth from home into homelessness, at that time among the devas the joyous utterance is proclaimed: 'A noble disciple intends to do battle with Mara.' This is the first joyous utterance proclaimed among the devas from time to time upon a certain occasion.

"Again, bhikkhus, at the time when a noble disciple lives engaged in cultivating the seven groups of the requisites of enlightenment, at that time among the devas the joyous utterance is proclaimed: 'A noble disciple is doing battle with Mara.' This is the second joyous utterance proclaimed among the devas from time to time upon a certain occasion.

"And again, bhikkhus, at the time when a noble disciple, through realization by his own direct knowledge, here and now enters and abides in the mind-release and wisdom-release that is taintless by the destruction of the taints, at that time among the devas the joyous utterance is proclaimed: 'A noble disciple has won the battle. He was in the forefront of the fight and he now dwells victorious.' This, bhikkhus, is the third joyous utterance proclaimed among the devas from time to time upon a certain occasion.

"These, bhikkhus, are the three joyous utterances proclaimed from time to time upon certain occasions."

This is the meaning of what the Lord said. So in regard to this it was said:

On seeing that he has won the battle,

Even the devas honour him,

The Fully Enlightened One's disciple,

A great one free from diffidence:

"We salute you, O thoroughbred man,

You who have won a difficult conquest.

Having routed the army of Death,

You are unhindered in liberation."

Thus do the devas extol him,

The one who has attained the goal,

For they do not perceive in him

Ground for subjection to Death's control.

This too is the meaning of what was said by the Lord, so I heard.

# FOR THE WELFARE OF MANY

This was said by the Lord, said by the Arahant, so I heard:

"Bhikkhus, these three persons appearing in the world appear for the welfare of many people, for the happiness of many people, out of compassion for the world, for the good, welfare, and happiness of devas and humans. What three?

"Here, bhikkhus, a Tathagata appears in the world, an Arahant, a Fully Enlightened One, possessing perfect knowledge and conduct, a sublime one, a world-knower, an unsurpassed leader of persons to be tamed, a teacher of devas and humans, an enlightened one, a Lord. He teaches Dhamma that is good at the outset, good in the middle, and good at the end, with its correct meaning and wording, and he proclaims the holy life in its fulfilment and complete purity. This, bhikkhus, is the first person appearing in the world who appears for the welfare of many people, for the happiness of many people, out of compassion for the world, for the good, welfare, and happiness of devas and humans.

"Next, bhikkhus, there is a disciple of that teacher, an arahant, one whose taints are destroyed, the holy life fulfilled, who has done what had to be done, laid down the burden, attained the goal, destroyed the fetters of being, and is completely released through final knowledge. He teaches Dhamma that is good at the outset, good in the middle, and good at the end, with its correct meaning and wording, and he proclaims the holy life in its fulfilment and complete purity. This, bhikkhus, is the second person appearing in the world who appears for the welfare of many people, for the happiness of many people, out of compassion for the world, for the good, welfare, and happiness of devas and humans.

"And next, bhikkhus, there is a disciple of that teacher, a learner who is following the path, who has learnt much and is of virtuous conduct. He teaches Dhamma that is good at the outset, good in the middle, and good at the end, with its correct meaning and wording, and he proclaims the holy life in its fulfilment and complete purity. This, bhikkhus, is the third person appearing in the world who appears for the welfare of many people, for the happiness of many people, out of compassion for the world, for the good, welfare, and happiness of devas and humans.

"These, bhikkhus, are the three persons appearing in the world who appear for the welfare of many people, for the happiness of many people, out of compassion for the world, for the good, welfare, and happiness of devas and humans."

This is the meaning of what the Lord said. So in regard to this it was said:

The teacher, the great sage,

Is the first in the world;

Following him is the disciple

Whose composure is perfected;

And then the learner training on the path,

One who has learnt much and is virtuous.

These three are chief amongst devas and humans:

Illuminators, preaching Dhamma,

Opening the door to the Deathless,

They free many people from bondage.

Those who follow the path

Well taught by the unsurpassed

Caravan-leader, who are diligent

In the Sublime One's dispensation,

Make an end of suffering

Within this very life itself.

This too is the meaning of what was said by the Lord, so I heard.

# FOREMOST FAITH

This was said by the Lord, said by the Arahant, so I heard:

"Bhikkhus, there are these three foremost kinds of faith. What are the three?

"Whatever beings there are, whether footless or two-footed or four-footed, with form or without form, percipient or non-percipient or neither-percipient-nor-non-percipient, of these the Tathagata is reckoned foremost, the Arahant, the Fully Enlightened One. Those who have faith in the Buddha have faith in the foremost, and for those with faith in the foremost the result will be foremost.

"Whatever states there are, whether conditioned or unconditioned, of these detachment is reckoned foremost, that is, the subduing of vanity, the elimination of thirst, the removal of reliance, the termination of the round (of rebirths), the destruction of craving, detachment, cessation, Nibbana. Those who have faith in the Dhamma of detachment have faith in the foremost, and for those with faith in the foremost the result will be foremost.

"Whatever communities or groups there are, bhikkhus, of these the Sangha of the Tathagata's disciples is reckoned foremost, that is, the four pairs of persons, the eight individuals. This Sangha of the Lord's disciples is worthy of gifts, worthy of hospitality, worthy of offerings, worthy of reverential salutation, the unsurpassable field of merit for the world. Those who have faith in the Sangha have faith in the foremost, and for those with faith in the foremost the result will be foremost.

"These, bhikkhus, are the three foremost kinds of faith."

This is the meaning of what the Lord said. So in regard to this it was said:

This is foremost for those with faith,

For those who know the foremost Dhamma:

Having faith in the Buddha as foremost,

Worthy of offerings, unsurpassed;

Having faith in the Dhamma as foremost,

The peace of detachment, bliss;

Having faith in the Sangha as foremost,

A field of merit unsurpassed.

Distributing gifts among the foremost,

Foremost is the merit that accrues;

Foremost their life and beauty,

Fame, reputation, happiness, and strength.

The wise one who gives to the foremost,

Concentrated on the foremost Dhamma,

Whether he becomes a deva or a human,

Rejoices in his foremost attainment.

This too is the meaning of what was said by the Lord, so I heard.

# LOVELY BEHAVIOUR

This was said by the Lord, said by the Arahant, so I heard:

"Bhikkhus, a bhikkhu who is of lovely behaviour, lovely nature, and lovely wisdom is called in this Dhamma-and-Discipline one who is fully accomplished, who has reached fulfilment, the supreme among humans.

"And how is a bhikkhu of lovely behaviour? Here, a bhikkhu is virtuous, he lives restrained by the restraint of the rules of discipline, endowed with perfect conduct and resort; seeing danger in the slightest faults, he undertakes the rules of training and trains in them. In this way a bhikkhu is one who is of lovely behaviour. Thus he is of lovely behaviour.

"And how is he of lovely nature? Here, a bhikkhu lives engaged in cultivating the seven groups of the requisites of enlightenment. In this way a bhikkhu is one who is of lovely nature. Thus he is of lovely behaviour and lovely nature.

"And how is he of lovely wisdom? Here, through realization by his own direct knowledge, a bhikkhu here and now enters and abides in the mind-release and wisdom-release that is taintless by the destruction of the taints. In this way a bhikkhu is one who is of lovely wisdom.

"Thus he is of lovely behaviour, lovely nature, and lovely wisdom. In this Dhamma-and-Discipline he is called one who is fully accomplished, who has reached fulfilment and is supreme among humans."

This is the meaning of what the Lord said. So in regard to this it was said:

A conscientious bhikkhu

Who never does wrong in any way,

Neither by body, speech, or mind,

Is called "one of lovely behaviour."

An unassuming bhikkhu

Who has cultivated well the states

That lead to enlightenment

Is called "one of lovely nature."

A taintless bhikkhu

Who understands for himself

The end of suffering here

Is called "one of lovely wisdom."

He who excels in these three things,

Untroubled, with doubt destroyed,

Unattached in all the world,

Is called "one who has abandoned all."

This too is the meaning of what was said by the Lord, so I heard.

# DECEITFUL

This was said by the Lord, said by the Arahant, so I heard:

"Bhikkhus, whatever bhikkhus are deceitful, stubborn, mere talkers, frauds, arrogant, and unconcentrated, these bhikkhus are no followers of mine. They have turned aside from this Dhamma-and-Discipline and will not achieve growth, progress, or development within it.

"But whatever bhikkhus are not deceitful, not mere talkers, wise, adaptable, and well concentrated, these bhikkhus are indeed my followers. They have not turned aside from this Dhamma-and-Discipline and will achieve growth, progress, and development within it."

This is the meaning of what the Lord said. So in regard to this it was said:

Deceitful, stubborn, mere talkers,

Frauds, arrogant, unconcentrated—

These make no progress in the Dhamma

Taught by the Fully Enlightened One.

Undeceitful, not talkative, wise,

Adaptable, well concentrated—

Such as these progress in the Dhamma

Taught by the Fully Enlightened One.

This too is the meaning of what was said by the Lord, so I heard.

# THE RIVER CURRENT

This was said by the Lord, said by the Arahant, so I heard:

"Suppose, bhikkhus, a man was being borne along by the current of a river that seemed pleasant and agreeable. But upon seeing him, a keen-sighted man standing on the bank would call out to him: 'Hey, good man! Although you are being borne along by the current of a river that seems pleasant and agreeable, lower down there is a pool with turbulent waves and swirling eddies, with monsters and demons. On reaching that pool you will die or suffer close to death.' Then, bhikkhus, upon hearing the words of that person, that man would struggle against the current with hands and feet.

"I have made use of this simile, bhikkhus, to illustrate the meaning. And this is the meaning here: 'The current of the river' is a synonym for craving. 'Seeming pleasant and agreeable' is a synonym for the six internal sense-bases. 'The pool lower down' is a synonym for the five lower fetters.'Turbulent waves' is a synonym for anger and frustration. 'Swirling eddies' is a synonym for the five strands of sensual pleasure. 'Monsters and demons' is a synonym for womenfolk. 'Against the current' is a synonym for renunciation. 'Struggling with hands and feet' is a synonym for instigating energy. 'The keen-sighted man standing on the bank' is a synonym for the Tathagata, the Arahant, the Fully Enlightened One."

This is the meaning of what the Lord said. So in regard to this it was said:

Desiring future security from bondage

One should abandon sensual desire

However painful this may be.

Rightly comprehending with wisdom,

Possessing a mind that is well released,

One may reach freedom step by step.

One who is a master of knowledge,

Who has lived the holy life,

Is called one gone to the world's end,

One who has reached the further shore.

This too is the meaning of what was said by the Lord, so I heard.

While Walking

This was said by the Lord, said by the Arahant, so I heard:

"Bhikkhus, if while walking a sensual thought or a thought of ill will or an aggressive thought arises in a bhikkhu, and if he tolerates it and does not reject it, does not dispel it and get rid of it and bring it to an end, that bhikkhu—who in such a manner is lacking in ardour and unafraid of wrongdoing—is called constantly lazy and indolent. If while standing a sensual thought or a thought of ill will or an aggressive thought arises in a bhikkhu, and if he tolerates it and does not reject it, does not dispel it and get rid of it and bring it to an end, that bhikkhu—who in such a manner is lacking in ardour and unafraid of wrongdoing—is called constantly lazy and indolent. If while sitting a sensual thought or a thought of ill will or an aggressive thought arises in a bhikkhu, and if he tolerates it and does not reject it, does not dispel it and get rid of it and bring it to an end, that bhikkhu—who in such a manner is lacking in ardour and unafraid of wrongdoing—is called constantly lazy and indolent. If while lying down a sensual thought or a thought of ill will or an aggressive thought arises in a bhikkhu, and if he tolerates it and does not reject it a sensual thought or a thought of ill will or an aggressive thought arises in a bhikkhu, and if he tolerates it and does not reject it, does not dispel it and get rid of it and bring it to an end, that bhikkhu—who in such a manner is lacking in ardour and unafraid of wrongdoing—is called constantly lazy and indolent. that bhikkhu is called constantly lazy and indolent.

"But if while walking ... standing ... sitting ... lying down a sensual thought or a thought of ill will or an aggressive thought arises in a bhikkhu and he does not tolerate it, but rejects it, dispels it, gets rid of it, and brings it to an end, that bhikkhu—who in such a manner is ardent and afraid of wrongdoing—is called constantly energetic and resolute."

This is the meaning of what the Lord said. So in regard to this it was said:

Whether walking or standing,

Sitting or lying down

Whoever thinks such thoughts

That are evil and worldly—

He is following a wrong path,

Infatuated with delusive things.

Such a bhikkhu cannot reach

Enlightenment which is supreme.

Whether walking or standing,

Sitting or lying down,

Whoever overcomes these thoughts,

Delighting in the quelling of thoughts—

Such a bhikkhu is able to reach

Enlightenment which is supreme.

This too is the meaning of what was said by the Lord, so I heard.

# THE WORLD

This was said by the Lord, said by the Arahant, so I heard:

"Bhikkhus, the world has been fully understood by the Tathagata; the Tathagata is released from the world. The origin of the world has been fully understood by the Tathagata; the origin of the world has been abandoned by the Tathagata. The cessation of the world has been fully understood by the Tathagata; the cessation of the world has been realized by the Tathagata. The course leading to the cessation of the world has been fully understood by the Tathagata; the course leading to the cessation of the world has been developed by the Tathagata.

"Bhikkhus, in the world with its devas, maras, and brahmas, with its recluses and brahmins, among humankind with its princes and people, whatever is seen, heard, sensed, cognized, attained, sought, and reflected upon by the mind—that is fully understood by the Tathagata: therefore he is called the Tathagata.

"Bhikkhus, from the night when the Tathagata awakened to unsurpassed full enlightenment until the night when he passes away into the Nibbana-element with no residue left, whatever he speaks, utters, and explains—all that is just so and not otherwise: therefore he is called the Tathagata.

"As the Tathagata says, so he does; as the Tathagata does, so he says: therefore he is called the Tathagata.

"In the world with its devas, maras, and brahmas, with its recluses and brahmins, among humankind with its princes and people, the Tathagata is the conqueror, unvanquished, all-seer, wielding power: therefore he is called the Tathagata."

This is the meaning of what the Lord said. So in regard to this it was said:

By knowledge of the whole world,

The whole world as it truly is,

He is released from all the world,

In all the world he is unattached.

The all-conquering heroic sage,

Freed from every bond is he;

He has reached that perfect peace,

Nibbana which is free from fear.

Rid of taints, he is enlightened,

Trouble-free, with doubts destroyed,

Reached the final end of deeds,

Released by clinging's full destruction.

The Enlightened One, the Lord,

A lion is he, unsurpassed;

For in the world together with its devas

He set the Brahma-wheel in motion.

Thus those devas and human beings,

Gone for refuge to the Buddha,

On meeting him pay homage to him,

The great one free from diffidence.

Tamed, of the tamed he is the best;

Calmed, of the calmed he is the seer;

Freed, of the freed he is the foremost;

Crossed, of the crossed he is the chief.

Thus do they pay him due homage,

The great one free from diffidence:

"In the world together with its devas

There is no person equalling you."

This too is the meaning of what was said by the Lord, so I heard.

The Book of the Buddha's Sayings is Finished.

# HUṀHUṄKASUTTA

### Whiny

So I have heard. At one time, when he was first awakened, the Buddha was staying near Uruvela at the goatherd's banyan tree on the bank of the Neranjara River. There the Buddha sat cross-legged for seven days without moving, experiencing the bliss of freedom. When seven days had passed, the Buddha emerged from that state of immersion.

Then a certain brahmin of the whiny sort went up to the Buddha and exchanged greetings with him. When the greetings and polite conversation were over, he stood to one side, and said, "Master Gotama, how do you define a brahmin? And what are the things that make one a brahmin?"

Then, understanding this matter, on that occasion the Buddha expressed this heartfelt sentiment:

"A brahmin who has banished bad qualities, —not whiny, not stained, but self-controlled, a complete knowledge master who has completed the spiritual journey— may rightly proclaim the brahmin doctrine, not proud of anything in the world."

# NANDASUTTA

## With Nanda

So I have heard. At one time the Buddha was staying near Savatthi in Jeta's Grove, Anathapindika's monastery. Now at that time Venerable Nanda, the Buddha's brother and maternal cousin, informed several mendicants: "I lead the spiritual life dissatisfied. I am unable to keep up the spiritual life. I shall resign the training and return to a lesser life."

Then a mendicant went up to the Buddha, bowed, sat down to one side, and told him what was happening.

So the Buddha addressed a certain monk, "Please, monk, in my name tell the mendicant Nanda that the teacher summons him." "Yes, sir," that monk replied. He went to Nanda and said to him, "Reverend Nanda, the teacher summons you."

"Yes, reverend," Nanda replied. He went to the Buddha, bowed, and sat down to one side. The Buddha said to him:

"Is it really true, Nanda, that you informed several mendicants that you are unable to keep up the spiritual life; that you shall resign the training and return to a lesser life?" "Yes, sir," he replied.

"But why are you so dissatisfied with the spiritual life?" "As I left my house, sir, the finest lady of the Sakyan land, her hair half-combed, glanced at me and said, 'Hurry back, master.' Recalling that, I am dissatisfied and shall resign the training."

Then the Buddha took Nanda by the arm and, as easily as a strong person would extend or contract their arm, vanished from Jeta's Grove and reappeared among the gods of the Thirty-Three.

Now at that time five hundred dove-footed nymphs had come to attend to Sakka, the lord of gods. Then the Buddha said to Nanda, "Nanda, do you see these five hundred dove-footed nymphs?" "Yes, sir," he replied.

"What do you think, Nanda? Who is more attractive, good-looking, and lovely—the finest lady of the Sakyan land, or these five hundred dove-footed nymphs?" "Compared to these five hundred dove-footed nymphs, the finest lady of the Sakyan land is like a deformed monkey with its ears and nose cut off. She doesn't count, there's no comparison, she's not worth a fraction. These five hundred dove-footed nymphs are far more attractive, good-looking, and lovely."

"Rejoice, Nanda, rejoice! I guarantee you five hundred dove-footed nymphs." "If, sir, you guarantee me five hundred dove-footed nymphs, I shall happily lead the spiritual life under the Buddha."

Then the Buddha took Nanda by the arm and, as easily as a strong person would extend or contract their arm, vanished from the gods of the Thirty-Three and reappeared at Jeta's Grove.

The mendicants heard, "It seems Venerable Nanda—who is both the Buddha's half-brother and maternal cousin—leads the spiritual life for the sake of nymphs. And it seems that the Buddha guaranteed him five hundred dove-footed nymphs."

Monks who were his friends accused him of being a hireling and a lackey, "It seems Nanda is a hireling, it seems he is a lackey: he leads the spiritual life for the sake of nymphs. And it seems that the Buddha guaranteed him five hundred dove-footed nymphs."

Then Nanda—embarrassed, ashamed, and disgusted at being called a hireling and a lackey—living alone, withdrawn, diligent, keen, and resolute, soon realized the supreme end of the spiritual path in this very life. He lived having achieved with his own insight the goal for which gentlemen rightly go forth from the lay life to homelessness. He understood: "Rebirth is ended; the spiritual journey has been completed; what had to be done has been done; there is no return to any state of existence." Venerable Nanda became one of the perfected.

Then, late at night, a glorious deity, lighting up the entire Jeta's Grove, went up to the Buddha, bowed, stood to one side, and said to him: "Sir, Venerable Nanda—who is both the Buddha's half-brother and maternal cousin—has realized the undefiled freedom of heart and freedom by wisdom in this very life. He lives having realized it with his own insight due to the ending of defilements." And the knowledge also came to the Buddha: "Nanda has realized the undefiled freedom of heart and freedom by wisdom in this very life. He lives having realized it with his own insight due to the ending of defilements."

Then, when the night had passed, Nanda went to the Buddha, bowed, sat down to one side, and said to him, "Sir, you guaranteed me five hundred dove-footed nymphs. I release you from that promise." "Nanda, I comprehended your mind and knew that you had realized the undefiled freedom of heart and freedom by wisdom. And deities also told me about this. As soon as your mind was freed from defilements by not grasping, I was released from that promise."

Then, understanding this matter, on that occasion the Buddha expressed this heartfelt sentiment:

"The mendicant who has crossed over the bog, who has crushed the thorns of sensuality, who has reached the end of delusion, trembles not at pleasure and pain."